MILES DAVIS Kind of Blue

D1545086

Contents:

Original vinyl release—Columbia CL 1355 (CS 8163-Stereo)

Trumpet—Miles Davis; Alto Saxophone—Julian "Cannonball" Adderley;
Tenor Saxophone—John Coltrane; Piano—Bill Evans; Bass—Paul Chambers;
Drums—Jimmy Cobb

Recorded at Columbia 30th Street Studio by Fred Plaut;
Original producer—Irving Townsend

Wynton Kelly replaces Evans on "Freddie Freeloader;"
Adderley does not play on "Blue in Green"

Cover Photo: Raymond Ross

ISBN 0-634-01169-3

HAL•LEONARD®
CORPORATION
7777 W. BLUEMOUND RD. P.O. BOX 13819 MILWAUKEE, WI 53213

Visit Hal Leonard Online at
www.halleonard.com

MILES DAVIS

Biography:

Miles Davis was one of the most important musicians in American music. An individual trumpet stylist, Miles Davis had more career highs than six giants of the music scene combined. He left many landmark recordings in a career that spanned bebop, cool jazz, modal jazz, fusion and hip-hop. He also promoted and discovered some of the most important musicians in the jazz world, including Bill Evans, John Coltrane, Red Garland, Chick Corea, Dave Liebman, Ron Carter, Wayne Shorter, and many, many others.

Miles Dewey Davis was born on May 25, 1926 in Alton, Illinois, but grew up in East St. Louis. He began playing trumpet when he was nine or ten. He went to New York in 1944 to study at the Juilliard School of Music, but he really wanted to be part of the jazz scene, so he dropped out after a few months. He played with Coleman Hawkins on recordings and gigs on 52nd Street, but by 1945 Miles was playing and recording with Charlie Parker. His style at that time was often tentative, but Parker and other musicians believed in him. Miles later gained valuable experience in the orchestra of Benny Carter on the West Coast, but he was back with Parker by 1948.

Miles took over a nine-piece rehearsal band with arrangements by Gerry Mulligan, Gil Evans, George Russell, John Lewis, and John Carisi in late 1948. It played one or two live gigs with varying personnel, but became famous as the "Birth of the Cool" ensemble based on twelve recordings for the Capitol label. These recordings highlighted a new approach to ensemble jazz and improvisation and continue to be influential.

Miles worked infrequently in the early '50s mainly due to a substance abuse problem, but he kicked the habit by 1954. An appearance at the Newport Jazz Festival in 1955 was a major success for him, and during this period he led a quintet featuring John Coltrane, Red Garland, Paul Chambers and Philly Joe Jones. Along with albums with this lineup which are now considered jazz classics, he began an association with composer/arranger Gil Evans that yielded several large orchestral albums garnering spectacular reviews and influencing players and composers worldwide. All of these albums have never been out of print.

In 1959, with an all-star ensemble of Coltrane, Chambers, Cannonball Adderley, Bill Evans, and Jimmy Cobb, Miles recorded the album *Kind of Blue*. This album became one of the most consistent selling albums in the history of the recording industry; it continues to sell 125,000 copies a year. The music on the album kick-started the modal jazz movement, and two of the five tunes became jazz standards.

By 1964, Davis was leading another incredible ensemble which included tenor saxophonist Wayne Shorter, keyboardist Herbie Hancock, bassist Ron Carter, and drummer Tony Williams. While still playing standard songs and new compositions, the group was looser and incorporated more modern and even avant-garde elements. The music continued to evolve, and by 1968, Davis encouraged the musicians to incorporate electronics and rock. Soon Chick Corea, bassist Dave Holland and drummer Jack DeJohnette were the featured players, and this ensemble was later known as one of the earliest 'fusion' ensembles. In fact, the double album *Bitches Brew* is cited as the recording that launched the fusion era of jazz. Long-time fans were confounded and alienated, but Miles pressed on in his new direction; his groups often included more than one guitar and/or keyboard. Miles was now controversial, and his live appearances were more popular with rock audiences than jazz fans. Ill health sidelined Davis in 1975, and for all intents and purposes, he'd retired. But in 1981, he was back with a group incorporating funk and modern pop music. One of the last concerts he played was a Quincy Jones-produced re-visit to the Birth of the Cool repertoire at the Montreux jazz festival. Miles died on September 28, 1991 in Santa Monica, California.

Kind of Blue

Background Notes:

One of the most influential albums in the history of jazz, Miles Davis' *Kind of Blue* was first released on August 17, 1959 and marked a major turning point for the music. With no rehearsal and the compositions basically sketches by Miles, the musicians created one of the landmarks in the new jazz of the '60s. The music has been called haunting, lyrical and hypnotic. Many musicians have credited the album with making them want to play jazz. Sales continue to astound the recording industry; reportedly, *Kind of Blue* sells about 125,000 copies a year worldwide.

Miles Davis was on a career high in 1959. After years of personal problems and low-profile gigs, Davis was now getting major attention. His small group and large ensemble albums (with arrangements by Gil Evans) were getting raves in the press. The members of the band on *Kind of Blue* were all-stars and leaders in their own right. Each had his own sound and approach, and yet this was definitely a cohesive band.

Kind of Blue represents some of the earliest examples of modal jazz, the tunes based more on scales than chords. The idea was to allow the players free reign to go in any number of melodic directions. In interviews, Miles stated how he felt modern jazz was becoming too harmony-oriented, and he looked to his music to open up more possibilities in melodic terms. He was a true visionary; modal jazz became more and more important as the sixties progressed.

Most of the compositions have become standards, and have even been used as teaching material.

All of these elements add up to a classic album, and now a classic music book.

About This Folio

The music was transcribed by Rob DuBoff, Mark Vinci, Mark Davis and Josh Davis. It is presented in transposed sketch score format. All ensemble lines and improvised solos are included. Rhythm section parts are often included as guides to give the "feel" of each composition. In addition to sections marked by letter, the number of each chorus is included. All of these decisions were made to address a number of uses.

1) For playing and performance by a sextet in the instrumentation matching the original.

2) For individual and class study.

SO WHAT

By MILES DAVIS

FREDDIE FREELOADER

By MILES DAVIS

BLUE IN GREEN

By MILES DAVIS

ALL BLUES

By MILES DAVIS

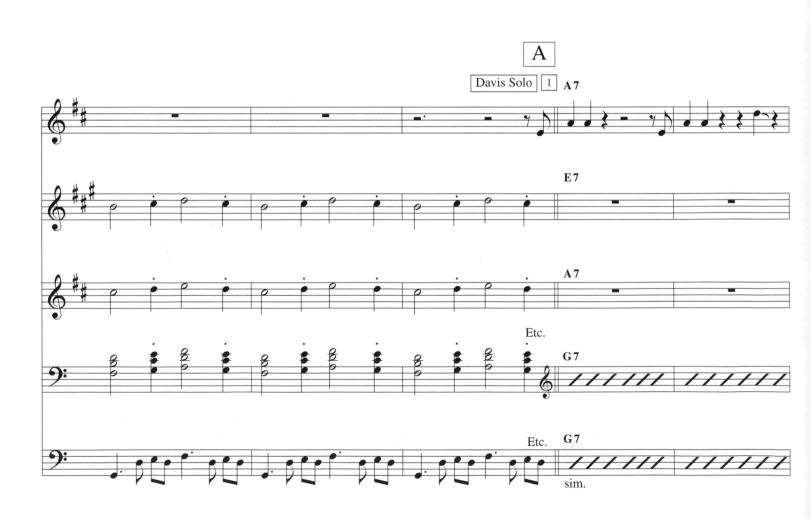

48

52

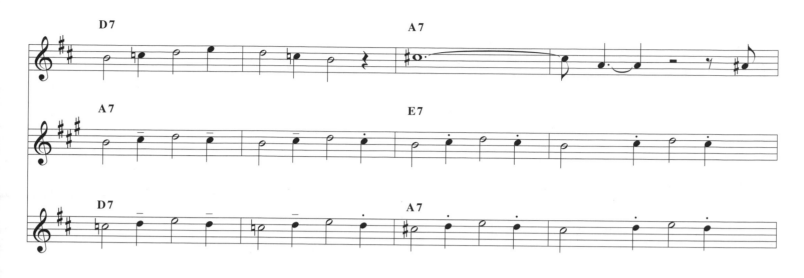

FLAMENCO SKETCHES

By MILES DAVIS

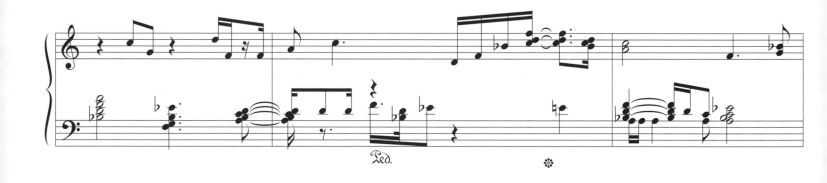

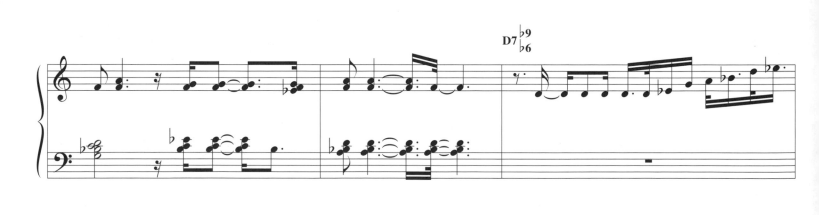

ARTIST TRANSCRIPTIONS®

Artist Transcriptions are authentic, note-for-note transcriptions of the hottest artists in jazz, pop, and rock today. These outstanding, accurate arrangements are in an easy-to-read format which includes all essential lines. Artist Transcriptions can be used to perform, sequence or reference.

GUITAR & BASS

The Guitar Book of Pierre Bensusan
00699072..$19.95

Ron Carter – Acoustic Bass
00672331..$16.95

Charley Christian –
The Art of Jazz Guitar
00026704 ....$6.95

Stanley Clarke Collection
00672307..$19.95

Larry Coryell – Jazz Guitar Solos
00699140..$9.95

Al Di Meola – Cielo E Terra
00604041..$14.95

Al Di Meola –
Friday Night in San Francisco
00660115..$14.95

Al Di Meola – Music, Words, Pictures
00604043..$14.95

Kevin Eubanks Guitar Collection
00672319..$19.95

The Jazz Style of Tal Farlow
00673245..$19.95

Bela Fleck and the Flecktones
00672359 Melody/Lyrics/Chords....$14.95

David Friesen – Departure
00673221..$14.95

David Friesen – Years Through Time
00673253..$14.95

Best Of Frank Gambale
00672336..$22.95

Jim Hall – Jazz Guitar Environments
00699389 Book/CD $19.95

Jim Hall – Exploring Jazz Guitar
00699306..$16.95

Scott Henderson Guitar Book
00699330..$19.95

Allan Holdsworth –
Reaching for the Uncommon Chord
00604049..$14.95

Leo Kottke – Eight Songs
00699215..$14.95

Wes Montgomery – Guitar Transcriptions
00675536..$14.95

Joe Pass Collection
00672353..$14.95

John Patitucci
00673216..$14.95

Django Reinhardt Anthology
00027083..$14.95

The Genius of Django Reinhardt
00026711..$10.95

Django Reinhardt – A Treasury of Songs
00026715..$12.95

John Renbourn – The Nine Maidens,
The Hermit, Stefan and John
00699071..$12.95

Great Rockabilly Guitar Solos
00692820..$14.95

John Scofield – Guitar Transcriptions
00603390..$16.95

Andres Segovia –
20 Studies for the Guitar
00006362 Book/Cassette $14.95

Johnny Smith Guitar Solos
00672374..$14.95

Mike Stern Guitar Book
00673224..$16.95

Mark Whitfield
00672320..$19.95

Jack Wilkins – Windows
00673249..$14.95

Gary Willis Collection
00672337..$19.95

CLARINET

Buddy De Franco Collection
00672423..$19.95

FLUTE

James Newton – Improvising Flute
00660108..$14.95

TROMBONE

J.J. Johnson Collection
00672332..$19.95

TRUMPET

Randy Brecker
00673234..$14.95

The Brecker Brothers...
And All Their Jazz
00672351..$19.95

Best of the Brecker Brothers
00672447..$19.95

Miles Davis – Originals
00672448..$19.95

Miles Davis – Standards
00672450..$19.95

Freddie Hubbard
00673214..$14.95

Tom Harrell Jazz Trumpet
00672382..$19.95

Jazz Trumpet Solos
00672363..$9.95

PIANO & KEYBOARD

Monty Alexander Collection
00672338..$19.95

Kenny Barron Collection
00672318..$22.95

Warren Bernhardt Collection
00672364..$19.95

Billy Childs Collection
00673242..$19.95

Chick Corea – Beneath the Mask
00673225..$12.95

Chick Corea – Elektric Band
00603126..$15.95

Chick Corea – Eye of the Beholder
00660007..$14.95

Chick Corea – Light Years
00674305..$14.95

Chick Corea – Paint the World
00672300..$12.95

Bill Evans Collection
00672365..$19.95

Benny Green Collection
00672329..$19.95

Ahmad Jamal Collection
00672322..$22.95

Jazz Master Classics for Piano
00672354..$14.95

Thelonius Monk – Intermediate
Piano Solos
00672392..$12.95

Jelly Roll Morton – The Piano Rolls
00672433..$12.95

Michel Petrucciani
00673226..$17.95

Bud Powell Classics
00672371..$19.95

André Previn Collection
00672437..$19.95

Joe Sample – Ashes to Ashes
00672310..$14.95

Horace Silver Collection
00672303..$19.95

Art Tatum Collection
00672316..$22.95

Art Tatum Solo Book
00672355..$19.95

Billy Taylor Collection
00672357..$24.95

McCoy Tyner
00673215..$14.95

SAXOPHONE

Julian "Cannonball" Adderly Collection
00673244..$16.95

Michael Brecker
00673237..$16.95

Michael Brecker Collection
00672429..$17.95

The Brecker Brothers...
And All Their Jazz
00672351..$19.95

Best of the Brecker Brothers
00672447..$19.95

Benny Carter Plays Standards
00672315..$22.95

Benny Carter Collection
00672314..$22.95

James Carter Collection
00672394..$19.95

John Coltrane – Giant Steps
00672349..$19.95

John Coltrane Solos
00673233..$22.95

Paul Desmond Collection
00672328..$19.95

Stan Getz
00699375..$14.95

Stan Getz – Bossa Novas – Saxophone
00672377..$16.95

Great Tenor Sax Solos
00673254..$18.95

Joe Henderson – Selections from
"Lush Life" & "So Near So Far"
00673252..$19.95

Best of Joe Henderson
00672330..$22.95

Jazz Master Classics for Tenor Sax
00672350..$18.95

Best Of Kenny G
00673239..$19.95

Kenny G – Breathless
00673229..$19.95

Kenny G – The Moment
00672373..$19.95

Joe Lovano Collection
00672326..$19.95

James Moody Collection – Sax and Flute
00672372..$19.95

The Art Pepper Collection
00672301..$19.95

Sonny Rollins Collection
00672444..$19.95

David Sanborn Collection
00675000..$14.95

Best of David Sanborn
00120891..$14.95

Stanley Turrentine Collection
00672334..$19.95

Ernie Watts Saxophone Collection
00673256..$18.95

FOR MORE INFORMATION, SEE YOUR LOCAL MUSIC DEALER,
OR WRITE TO:

HAL•LEONARD® CORPORATION

7777 W. BLUEMOUND RD. P.O. BOX 13819 MILWAUKEE, WI 53213

Visit our web site for a complete listing of our titles with songlists.
www.halleonard.com